AMAZON BOOK SELLING GUIDE
The Most Effective Way to Sell on Amazon

Thomas Van

DEDICATION

This book is dedicated to the entrepreneurs out there looking for a better way to earn a living. For the brave few that want to be more than just another employee. For those seeking financial freedom. For those looking to earn some extra money. For all those open-minded hard-working individuals, I dedicate this book to you.

Contents

ACKNOWLEDGMENTS

This book couldn't have come to be without the hard work and patience of Kathi who is always open and supportive of my new "crazy" ideas. Thanks for going on the road with me and helping build our business together. I know it wasn't easy working from sunup till sundown for days at a time.

I would also like to thank the random strangers on the Internet that take time out of their day to brainstorm and discuss new ways to make money. If it wasn't for the Tik-Tok videos and reddit posts I may have never stumbled upon this business.

INTRODUCTION

Whether you're looking to sell books on Amazon, Amazon FBA, eBay, or some other market place this guide will help you build your business from the ground up. Using the information in this guide will help you make a part-time or full-time income from thrifting books to resell online.

Thanks to Tik/Tok, YouTube, and other platforms, book selling usually makes the list of top ways to make money on the side. If you're reading this guide you're probably pumped about the idea and ready to get started.

You've made a good choice; this little book is packed with essential information that will save you months of trial and error.

Before starting you should know that there is a lot of bad/misinformation out there about book selling. This is not an easy way to make money fast. It can be competitive and if you don't enjoy the aspects of this business, you won't make it that far. If you're a motivated individual or an individual that realistically approaches book selling looking for some side cash, then you're in the right spot.

Most of the videos on book selling are typically made by people who are naturally good at running businesses and can outsource all the hard work to others. Some of them have a direct play in the book selling business. They could be generating a large portion of their money from an app, a spreadsheet, a course, or some other piece of software or equipment that book sellers "need".

If it's not one of those things then they could be gathering revenue from channel views across YouTube, TikTok, Instagram, Facebook, etc. Just be aware that they could be generating revenue from other sources beyond book selling. Some of them may not even sell books anymore if they ever did.

These types of people will have some level of success in just about any business they run and if you're one of those people then I would consider just skimming this guide and then jumping right into producing the content they are. I don't want you to be fooled into thinking they are becoming rich and famous by doing all the work themselves or from just book selling. Some of them have teams and a variety of support staff that help with the process.

Their format usually involves a large network of resources and contacts, even book scouts, and more closely resembles running your own Multilevel Marketing (MLM) Business than just an individual going out on their own trying to make a living.

In this business there is room for the part-time solo individual, the full-time worker, the small business owner, and the large business owner. It scales as far as you want it to.

This guide is mainly for those who want to be self-employed. Those that want to make enough money to live off which usually becomes a full-time job. If you prefer to set your own hours, make a little (or a lot of) side cash, and be your own boss -- then this guide applies directly to you.

A common misconception is that book selling depends on the area you live in. I have found this to be entirely false. This stuff can be done anywhere.

You don't need to live in a big city with major thrift stores that have bins filled with books sold by the pound to work this business. I have also found that you can be successful hitting up the ma and pa thrift shops in rural areas because they usually lack competition. Making driving routes of all these stores, even if you travel a couple hundred miles a day, can really pay out.

For most of these places you'll be the first book scouter they've ever seen, not to mention the prices are astronomically better than a place like Goodwill.

A lot of people are deterred from this type of business because they feel awkward going book by book scanning and looking them up while other people are standing there watching them wondering what they are doing. People will approach you and ask why you're scanning or what you're doing and it's important to recognize that this could lead into a 30-minute conversation which you don't have time for.

I have a basic response when store employees or other shoppers ask me what I'm doing. I tell them I am a book collector and I'm looking for specific books. I have an app on my phone that knows what books I need to complete the collections so when I scan them it tells me if I need them or not. This usually suffices.

If you tell them you are an online bookseller, you could lead yourself into a long conversation about profits and the business --- a conversation that you don't want to be in.

The last thing you want to do is give the manager the idea of just selling their books online like a lot of Goodwills do. Be careful what information you give out if you want to keep coming back to the same stores.

Having gone over all of that, we will proceed into the getting started section which will cover all the things you will want to have BEFORE you get started. These things are not required but will help save time, money, and increase profits.

Come along and I'll walk you through the business and you can decide if it's right for you.

FROM MY PERSONAL EXPERIENCE

Be wary of "ghost" entrepreneurs. Ghost entrepreneurs have little knowledge or expertise in the businesses they create. This business model has always existed, but it really started to crop up online when affiliate marketing started to hit a high with digital products in the early 2000's.

Back then, I had a small team building strategy guides in the video game industry to sell as digital products. Our big guide took up most of our time with updates and was considered the most popular guide at the time. Every person on my team played the game at least 8 hours a day competitively and knew what they were doing.

Then one day we started getting competition from an unknown person. After checking out their products, we saw a bunch of sub-par products being produced in mass, not just for our specific game but for at least a dozen games, all done by a single person.

It turned out this person was basically taking stuff from existing guides, sometimes rewriting it, and compiling his own compendiums to try and sell in the marketplace as his own products. While he never became a top seller with any of them, he sold enough to be deemed a "success" completely faking and counterfeiting his way to fame.

When digital products for those specific games started to decline, he then built an affiliate marketing course and claimed himself a successful entrepreneur. He somehow has a following and produces videos and sells courses on that topic now.

There are good, legitimate, helpful people in this business who produce quality content, but there are also people producing content like the person I mentioned above. Some people run from hot trend to hot trend throwing spaghetti at the wall to see what sticks so they can make a quick buck off people and move on.

Their expertise is in making professional looking content, marketing material, and products. They often use templates and have everything in place so that they can jump from market to market and all they need to do is use someone else's content and hard work to make their content and launch their business.

CHAPTER 1: GETTING STARTED

THE JOURNEY OF A THOUSAND MILES BEGINS WITH A SINGLE STEP – LAO TZU

The process of selling books goes like this: acquire books, prepare books for sale, list books for sale, ship to customers/Amazon, and profit.

Sounds simple right?

Well it can be a bit overwhelming when you get going so here are some things that can make your life easier at each step of the way.

ACQUIRING BOOKS

For book sourcing you will need a phone, a scouting app, and a Bluetooth handheld scanner to optimally function.

Any type of smartphone that isn't slow and old will work. It must have Bluetooth capability and data (or in store Wi-Fi). I use an iPhone because that's my preference.

You will be using either the phones camera or a Bluetooth scanner to scan the barcode, ISBN, or title off each book.

You will have to install an app on your phone that will take your scanned barcodes or ISBNs and check them against Amazon's database to calculate profit after fees.

Of course, you can do this without a Bluetooth scanner just using your phone camera and using the free Amazon Sellers app to look up items, but the process is neither fast nor efficient. By the time you decide you're going to take a book using this method I will have scanned the entire store and be onto the next one with a cart load of books.

It's important to get a Bluetooth scanner and an app.

There are several apps to choose from. I use ScoutIQ because it lets me customize triggers. Triggers are used to alert you of keepers while you scan. It also comes with default trigger settings that work well for beginners.

Apps like ScoutIQ make things easier because they look up all the book listings and their fees while calculating your potential profit. You can do the math and guesswork in your head, but it will slow you down no matter how quick you are.

It doesn't matter what app you use, just make sure it takes your scans via Bluetooth scanner and has the ability to use your camera to read ISBNs off a book AND calculates your profit by taking the sell price minus all fees.

With a scanner I've been able to scan over 3000 books in a single day (during store hours) mainly because I didn't have to use my phone camera on the books with barcodes. It's a lot easier to just hit it with a scanner like you're working a self-checkout system at a store.

If you are lucky enough to find books with barcodes that aren't covered up by stickers you could easily scan 3000 books an hour.

The goal with a Bluetooth scanner is to get one small enough that you can hold it easily in your hand with your phone. It's a good idea to get some 3M Velcro tape and attach the scanner right to the back of your phone case so that the phone and scanner are basically one unit: point, scan, and click.

ScoutIQ lets you know that it's accepted by a ding sound or you can look at the screen while you scan. If you want to be hardcore, get some headphones, hold the scanner in your hand, keep your phone in your pocket, and listen for the dings. I don't prefer this method because I like to make sure the "accept" is legit, more on that later.

I also like to conceal my scanner underneath my phone so to normal people walking by it just looks like I'm looking through books while holding my phone. I'm so good at concealing what I'm doing that you would have to stand there and watch me for a while to catch a glimpse of the scanner. Normally my girlfriend gets all the attention and people ask her what she's doing while I'm hammering away on books giggling to myself. She's way better looking than I am, so it may not actually be the concealed scanner keeping people away from me, but I like to think I'm operating in stealth mode anyway. Whether I'm concealed or she's a decoy the result is I get to keep scanning uninterrupted.

These are all the basic things you will need at a minimum to get serious about scanning books. Now let's head into what is needed to prep the books you find.

PREPARING BOOKS

I put a few things together because you'll likely do all of this in the same place once you take your books back to your homemade shipping center or storage area.

To prepare your books you will likely be cleaning them up, removing stickers, and sometimes fixing binding or pages.

Using **Elmer's Craft Bond** can help you reattach loose pages or fix loose binding. Practice on some junk books first so you don't end up ruining your profitable ones on accident.

It's not worth it to try to repair a book unless it has a high profit margin. For me that's $20 or more because sometimes the repair is an intense operation that can use up a lot of time, especially on your first few attempts.

Repairing books is an acquired skill that takes practice. The art of book repair goes beyond this guide but a quick search on "how to repair a book binding" "how to reattach a loose page" or "how to repair books" will get you to the right type of guides for this process.

Goo Gone Adhesive Remover is also another item you should get. Even if you peel the sticker off or wipe it off there will usually be a residue left that water/soap can't get off.

Be careful about using water on paper-based covers that aren't protected by a finish or plastic film. Some of them look like they can take a bit of water, but you'll find that it absorbs into the material and either stains or chews a hole through your book. Messing up sticker removal is a good way to reduce the value of your book.

For peeling stickers, you will have the option of plastic or metal tools. The plastic tools seem to wear out or bend frequently. They make a plastic razor model that has replacement "blades" that can be swapped when they get worn out. Others are single units, but I've found those wear out fast as well.

Using a metal remover is a very precise skill (yes, I learned the hard way). Pushing too hard (which really isn't that hard at all) can result in peeling, tearing, or ripping of the book cover. Sometimes with a metal remover you think you're just getting the sticker off and realize you've taken the cover with it. Other things to watch out for with a metal remover is cutting yourself. If it slips off the sticker (has happened to me more than once) and hits your hands or fingers it's like smashing a razor into it, instant cut.

I recommend having both tools on hand, but I also recommend being very careful and to never apply too much pressure. Work slowly until you acquire enough knowledge and skill to know which tool works best on what type of stickers and covers.

Some people have had great success using a heat gun or hair dryer to heat the sticker up before peeling it off. This is another option available to you.

The safest method of removing stickers I've found is to dab a washcloth rag into some water and lightly press on the sticker while rubbing the cloth in circles. When you perfect this method, the sticker will eventually start to flake off. Then dab the cloth into some Goo Gone and finish off the residue.

Be careful with the water method if you've attempted to use a tool to remove the sticker. Using a tool can leave small scuffs on the surface of the cover that will cause the water / rubbing to also tear into the cover more.

There are stickers that you will never want to remove from books. These include stickers not on the cover, library stickers, stickers from bookstores, and some price stickers.

The ONLY stickers I remove are price stickers and ONLY if the price showing is less than what I list it for. You probably don't want to sell a book for $50 that you ship out with a 25-cent garage sale sticker on it.

On the opposite hand, sending books out with higher priced stickers may have the opposite effect where the customer feels like they got a good deal for the price they paid.

Imagine the conversation they have with their friends.

"Hey Larry, check out this $50 book I just got off Amazon for $8."
"Wow! That's a pretty sweet deal Tina."

There are condition notes for library books and books with writing or stickers on the inside pages. I have found that attempting to remove these stickers will quickly damage your book to the point where it would be embarrassing to sell.

Remember, there isn't a noticeable price difference between the conditions of books below $25 so don't waste time trying to remove impossible stickers.

Other things you'll have to watch out for are highlighting and writing, these books can still be listed if the condition and details of the listing follow Amazons guidelines.

It is possible to remove pencil markings with an eraser but for the most part, unless it's a $50 book or more, it's simply not worth the effort to try to remove anything.

When I first started out I tried to remove every sticker and fix every book up so that it was in the best condition possible and in that process I learned that I was wasting my time and in a lot of cases making the book worse.

Write in the condition notes and just send it!

LISTING BOOKS

If you're going to sell on Amazon remember to upgrade your account to a professional seller account, if you don't, they will charge you an extra $1 per book sale. You will also need this type of account to get your book scanning app to sync up with Amazon's database. If you aren't using an app yet, for whatever reason, you should still have an Amazon Professional Sellers account. Even though it currently costs $40 a month you should be selling at least 40 books a month to make up for it.

The best way to list on Amazon is to get an app that will help you list in mass. You can always use the Amazon App to list books if you wish, but this can be time consuming. I use Scanlister but there are others out there I haven't used. It doesn't matter what app you use as long as you have an app and it allows you to scan books into a big list, set prices, set conditions, set details, and create a shipment for you to send to Amazon with a single click.

You can send up to 50lbs of books in one box to Amazon warehouses. When I first started out listing on Amazon, I used the seller's app and took pictures of every book and its flaws (silly me). It took forever and I was about to quit before I finally realized almost nobody else was doing this unless there's something major that needs to be documented about a book.

Not many people care about pictures or even read the condition notes.

The book details seem to be there to protect yourself in case a customer returns a product and leaves a bad review. Not that Amazon will help or care but at least then you can say, "Hey, look I listed that flaw in the notes before they bought it". At least then you can pretend to feel better about a customer that didn't do any due diligence.

In your listing app you will only need to set the condition: acceptable, good, very good, like new, etc. In addition to that condition there are other details that some of the apps have included by default like "contains highlighting" "minimal wear" "contains writing" etc. These can be modified and edited to whatever you like. Listing with an app should be quick and easy.

You will also have the option to provide labels for your books or have Amazon label them for you. A label is required so that the book can be found in the warehouse. If you choose to let Amazon label for you, as of right now it will cost you $.30 per book. If you decide to do it yourself, you can get a label printer that will print off the books labels as you scan them into your listing software.

I chose to make my own labels and I use a DYMO 4XL that is setup with Scanlister to print a label each time I scan a book in. Then I put the label on the book and then put the book in the box. A cheaper option is the DYMO Labelwriter 450 if you're not going to be high volume.

The only annoying thing I have found in this process is that I also use my Dymo to print shipping labels and those use different label sizes than the book labels, so I switch between rolls. To solve this issue, they make a Dymo Labelwriter 450 Twin Turbo that holds two different types of labels and can print shipping labels off one side and book labels off another side if you set it up that way. **The shipping labels are 4x6 and the book labels are 2 ¼ by 1 ¼ inches.**

If you are going to be doing all the shipping yourself, you will only need shipping labels, but you will also want to get a bunch of poly lined bubble mailers. I've found that **8.5" x 12" mailers** seem to work for most books, and I keep a large supply of those for my eBay and Merchant Fulfilled sales.

If you decide to go with Amazon's FBA (which you should definitely consider) you will want to acquire small shipping boxes from U-Haul, Menards, Home Depot, Lowes, or any other type of store that provides these boxes. You can also buy your boxes online at Amazon or Uline. The typical dimensions are around **12x12x16 or 14x14x14.** These size boxes seem to be perfect for keeping your shipment below the maximum of 50lbs per box while still filling the entire box with books.

THE MARKETPLACES

You will be using Amazon to be successful in the book business, however, there are scenarios where it makes sense to sell on eBay or Facebook (FB) Marketplace. You may want to sell on eBay or FB Marketplace if you've acquired a classic or rare book that doesn't have any listings on Amazon or wouldn't make sense to sell on Amazon. You could also sell on eBay or FB if you have a collection of fiction or other books by the same author or same genre that could be sold as a set or lot.

Amazon is great for individual books or "real sets". If the set or collection doesn't have an ISBN, it's a no go. However, there are books that won't do well on Amazon that you could package into a collection or lot and sell on eBay for a premium price. It could be a collection based on genres like "self-help" or "sci-fi fantasy". It could be a grouping of similar authors or the same author or even selling books off a list could be profitable, i.e., "Top 10 Books That Will Change Your Life". There are a lot of ways to make money grouping books to sell on eBay or FB Marketplace locally that won't work on Amazon, so get creative!

There are specific reasons for selling on other marketplaces but if you're going to be selling in mass, Amazon has the most market share for book selling. There are successful sellers on eBay or people that claim it's "where the parties at", however, eBay in no way shape or form can even come close to the amount of exposure you will get on Amazon. Amazon has around three times the daily audience as eBay and a case could be made that the book audience on Amazon is larger than all of eBay combined.

When people think of buying the next best seller, eBay is not at the top of the list on where to find it, UNLESS, the book is not available on Amazon or other sites. eBay is good for specialty items. Got an autographed book, a collector's edition, a rare find, or a classic book? eBay is probably better suited to find a unique buyer for you.

Let's try to be realistic. Selling 100 books a day on eBay wouldn't be as satisfying as selling 100 books a day on Amazon. Amazon has the capability to handle all your customer service and shipping while eBay does not. This allows you to scale on Amazon and just sit back and collect a paycheck. eBay is like fulfilling orders yourself on Amazon, it's a good mix to have, but easy to grow too large for just one person to handle. Amazon's FBA is the way to go if you're doing this solo or with a partner and want to automate the process so you can focus on sourcing books instead.

RESEARCHING BOOKS

Sometimes you come across a book that's hard to find an accurate or true value for. Below are several tools you can use to get additional pricing information when Amazon fails you.

Bookfinder.com

This is where to go when you've found a book that won't face scan, has no ISBN, or won't show up by title in your book scouting app. You can search by author, title, or ISBN. When you find the book, it will show you all of the prices and where it's for sale. This tool can be used to help you find pricing information on rare or odd books. It may also be of use in finding other versions of a book with the same title, for example, Treasure Island seems to have over 50 different publications.

Sellbackyourbook.com

This is another tool you can utilize. Instead of shipping your book off to Amazon or trying to sell it you can simply sell it to these guys and be done with it. This will also give you a base value for your book as both a buyer and as a reseller. It will show you what they will pay for the book (you shouldn't be paying more than this when you source it if possible) and they will tell you how much you can buy the book for which is useful because you're going to be selling it.

eBay.com

Going to eBay.com or using the eBay app will let you search for almost anything but when you put the sold items filter on, it will tell you exactly what the item sold for and when. This will help you price a book if you plan to sell it on eBay or other marketplaces. This can be useful if you have trouble locating a book or if it's a restricted item on Amazon that you don't have permission to sell. Sometimes selling restricted books is easier on eBay instead.

Keepa.com

Keepa gives you access to Amazon pricing history. This can be integrated right into your ScoutIQ app so you can view price history graphs on the spot. It is worth the extra money for premium data access via monthly subscription. This tool will save you from making many mistakes.

When you come across a book that doesn't have a lot of listings, there might be one person listing a $10 book for $400 just to see if it will sell, but the historical data may show this book only sells for around $10.

Without checking the historical pricing data, you may overpay for this book or think you picked up a gem when it's just a desperate seller or two having the only listings and messing around with the prices.

THE TOTAL COST TO START

You've probably figured out that doing this business without limiting yourself is going to cost you a bit of money. Assuming you already have a phone and cell service, we are talking about an initial startup fee for shipping supplies, cleaning supplies, a scanner, and a label printer at easily over $200 with some replenishment expenses for labels, boxes, tape, etc.

You will also be looking at a monthly subscription fee for scanning software, listing software, an Amazon Seller Account, and repricers of $100-150 a month. You can save on almost all these expenses until you see if the business is feasible for you. ScoutIQ offers a 14-day trial and so do some of the other scanning software. Activate this free trial and buy a Bluetooth scanner off Amazon. Go out for the next 2 weeks and see how many books you can find.

If you are unable to find enough, no problem, let your trial expire and return your scanner to Amazon for a full refund. Remember to at least find a few thousand books to scan before you throw in the towel, this is really a numbers game mixed with some overall strategy. Don't forget to take the time and drive to neighboring cities, search for different thrift stores, and see what you can find.

This isn't an easy job so don't go out for an hour, scan, and call it quits. You really should scan several thousand books across different stores and even different cities to see if it's feasible. You can use this time to watch for other people scanning and talk to the employees to figure out when books are restocked. If possible, do your trial period across yard/garage sale season just in case you're in an area where book scouting only works as a seasonal job. You can always activate your accounts and software for just the warm months and take the rest of the time off if so.

CHAPTER 2: SOURCING BOOKS

IF THINGS WERE EASY TO FIND, THEY WOULDN'T BE WORTH FINDING – TOM HANKS

There are a lot more thrift stores than you may think. If you aren't already using it, I recommend downloading the google maps app onto your phone and just typing the word thrift and searching your location. Oftentimes in small cities you'll find up to a dozen additional thrift stores in the same cities as the main ones like Goodwill. Don't use the regular maps program included in iOS, for some reason it wouldn't show me the other thrift stores or would randomly show me whatever it felt like. It even omitted some of the bigger stores that I ended up finding later so use at your own risk.

Even in small towns that don't have a Goodwill you'll usually find some hidden treasures or locally run thrift shops. These can net you major finds and profits, usually only once every few months, but if you find enough of them you can put them in rotation. Sometimes it's like coming up on a small gold mine. There's usually no competition in the area because you can't make a full-time job thrifting just a few small stores. It's a perfect opportunity for the person willing to drive a few hundred miles at a time.

This allows you to string a series of these stores together that can be quite profitable even after gas and hotels are taken out of the expenses.

Some of these smaller thrift stores have abnormal or short hours. Sometimes it's 9-4pm only and some of them are only open on certain days. Getting a notebook and making a logbook of every store you go to will help you plan future visits. It helps a lot if you ask an employee or manager when they usually put out their books. I've ran across some stores that only restock once a month. Having the right restock time and dates will allow you to show up first.

Asking simple questions can give you an opportunity to get to know the staff better and for the non-big brand thrift stores, you'll find it's much easier to build a relationship and get back room access to their books BEFORE they put them out. Most of the time the smaller thrift shop owners are grateful to have any business at all and you are doing them a favor by going through a massive pile of books in their back rooms.

Don't forget to take out your logbook and mark the date of the trip, the location, the store hours, and any other unique characteristics of the store so that you remember the important details clearly. Things like: "small store, only 50 books total, don't come here again." can be very helpful in future planning. After you've done as many stores as I have you start to get the locations mixed up and can't remember what each store looked like.

Sometimes you can use google to find pictures of the store to get an idea of the layout before you get there. Some stores are surprisingly huge. One of the stores I frequent has a used book section half the size of a Barnes and Noble. If you don't plan your trip right, it's easy to end up not having enough time to complete the store before it closes. Always arrange your trip by location and store hours and make sure you leave yourself enough time to complete a store. I'm usually on a tight schedule and can't return to finish scans the next day.

If I show up to a store at 3pm and it closes at 4pm then I've given myself only an hour to complete the scan. Once 4pm hits I'm on the road to another town 30 miles away to finish a store that closes by 7pm. It could be a month or more before I come back to that store. Due to poor planning, I've likely left some money behind.

Preparing for a Road Trip

Even if you don't think you're going on a road trip you should always be prepared. In this business we don't work 9-5, we work when there is money to be made and sometimes that entails being on the road for a few days at a time. For the part-timers, there are still things in this prep list for you.

Carry Cash

Some stores you encounter may not take debit/credit cards or their systems could be down. I grew up in a rural area where we still barely have internet in some places, so I'm used to having to pay with cash. Bring a few hundred dollars with, you can always put it back into your account later.

Pack phone/scanner chargers

When you're going hardcore scan mode you can run an iPhone battery out before you're ready to call it quits. Scanners are usually harder to run out in a single day, but you'll want extra power sources. Try to charge in the car from store to store to keep your battery levels up. Bring a backup phone / scanner if you can afford it. The last thing you want to do is be 100 miles from home with no way to charge your devices.

Download Your Database

Most Amazon scouting apps have an offline / database mode, if you don't have one, get one. You can download the entire Amazon database on your phone before you go thrifting. You may be thinking "Oh this isn't an issue in my area because I live in a city and we have Wi-Fi everywhere."

Cool story bro!

I used to think like that until I entered the basement of a church thrift shop and found the cell service doesn't reach down into the dungeon. I've also encountered this issue in metal buildings where I've had good service outside the store, but inside the store, no service for the book section. I had to grab books and go to another section of the store to scan and it took forever.

Good gas mileage / storage

This was written during the pandemic timeframe and gas isn't really an issue because it's cheap right now, but in normal times it can add up. In addition to gas, you should have adequate vehicle storage. I've filled up an entire minivan with books in a day trip and I only have the two front seats in it. Keep in mind that any car can pull a 4x6 trailer and getting a hitch setup is only a few hundred dollars. This would enable you to find a trailer to borrow or pull on your trips if storage is an issue. A new 4x6 enclosed trailer is only around $1500 or less, if it lets you get an extra thousand books a trip it will pay for itself quickly.

Ship on the Go

Yes, you read that right. Consider shipping boxes to Amazon on the go. All you need to do is bring some sticker removal tools, your DYMO printer, a laptop, a few boxes, and some packaging tape. If you are on the road and at full capacity but still have more to do --- it is completely acceptable to dump off a bunch of books to Amazon and make them label them for you (30 cents per book at the time of this writing). UPS stores are abundant, even small towns have a place to ship from. At the end of the day, pull some labels off, scan your books into your listing tool, throw them in a box, and ship them to Amazon. I usually get around 50 books in a box which will cost about $15 for Amazon to label them. The cost is irrelevant compared to the amount of money you will lose if you stop scanning.

Supplies and Clothes

"Oh, you don't need to bring anything to eat or any clothes to wear, this is going to be a short trip," said myself TO myself.

Three days later I pull into my driveway wearing the same clothes and half dead from starvation. I take this stuff seriously. I'm the type of person that will pull up google maps and check thrift shops within 100 miles and keep going until I've done them all. When I get to the edge of the 100 miles, I'll do it again and go to those thrift stores. When I'm finished, I'm usually far away from home and living in a minivan. I don't stop easily when I'm on a roll. I've even bought some clothes to wear from the thrift stores to prolong my trip.

About Goodwill

When people think of acquiring books from thrift stores, they usually think of Goodwill. In my experience, Goodwill is one of the worst thrift stores to acquire books from. When I am on a sourcing trip I will only go to a Goodwill if I have had a positive experience at a specific store before or I have gone through every other thrift store and there is nothing left.

The best thing about Goodwill is that it's typically open way later than other thrift stores. Unfortunately, the price of books at Goodwill has gotten so insane that even though you can find a few good picks or have a good trip it really rips into your available cash.

Buying too many books from Goodwill usually comes at a cost. Too many books from Goodwill can deplete your cash and keep you from finishing the more lucrative thrift stores. This is a big deal for me because I often travel hours away from home at a time. The price of books at Goodwill in my small town range from $2-3 per book which isn't bad. But as you head into larger cities, they can range from $5-7.

Not a big deal if you're making money, right? Think again.

Most scouting apps have default triggers that take into consideration the cost of a book and will show accepted books with a $2-3 profit. That means if a book has a cost of $5 at Goodwill and has a $2 profit, the software will tell you to "accept" or get the book. Cool you've made money --- but at what cost?

You've spent $5 to make $2, that's only a 40% return! In most cases this isn't bad but what if you only had $100 to spend on a thrifting trip? Most of us aren't strapped with cash to make such a bad investment on a book from Goodwill --- my typical short trips are limited to $500-$800 to acquire books.

If you spend $100 at Goodwill, you'll be out of cash quickly and end up with only 20 books. With a $2 profit on each you're looking at a $40 return on your $100. High book prices really stink.

You could modify your triggers to only take books with a $5 profit, but it will significantly reduce the number of books you get by at least 10x. It's probably not even worth trying to thrift for most people at that point. If you were able to find 20 books for $5 each with a $2 profit, you'd be lucky if 1-2 of those 20 books had a $5 or larger profit.

We need huge returns and trailer loads of books. There are a lot of other thrift stores that have bigger book selections than Goodwill and the cost of books range from $1-2. In March I acquired about one thousand books with an average cost of $1.50. When you spend $1.50 per book and you are still making at least $2-3 profit that's a huge return on your initial investment.

That's why it's vital to find a decent priced thrift store. Goodwill has no special books, they are literally (no pun intended) the same books that other thrift stores have. Each place is going to have a few hidden gems but only looking for the big profit books is not a sustainable business model, it's a treasure hunt. If you're looking to pay some bills, then shopping at a decently priced store means you'll always leave with some profit.

If you are limited to $100 would you rather have 100 books at $1 each or 20 books at $5 each? We're talking about a profit of at least $200 off the 100 books or a profit of only $40 off the 20 books. Do you see why Goodwill is a last resort stop?

One thing people fail to recognize is that no matter how hard we try to pick the best books, sometimes we make an error, or our scouting app gives us misleading information. If one or more of the books you have are duds, would you want a $1 dud or a $5 dud from Goodwill? How about if someone returns an item?

I don't care as much about returns because I only paid $1 for the book but when you're paying $5 per book that can add up quick. Sometimes people will leave you a good review from a bad scenario. I pay so little for books that whenever someone has an issue or wants a refund, I just send them a refund and tell them to keep the book.

While you're looking for your $50 profit book in Goodwill, I've already acquired 100 books in the same time frame that will bring me 4x the profit with less risk. I want to make the best use of my time and while treasure hunting is fun and exciting, I want to make sure I reach my baseline profit each month before I go out on too many treasure hunts.

As you've learned by now, I am a hardcore rural scanner that is making a living doing this. My primary acquisition source is thrifting; however, I started my journey on FB Marketplace and you should be aware of other places to source from.

Other Ways to Acquire Books

Facebook Marketplace

When I started out, I didn't think I would ever have to go into a thrift store because I was making so much money off textbooks on Facebook Marketplace. That dream ended when the supply in my area ran out. A lot of people selling on Facebook Marketplace are aware of how much their book should be worth. Some of them will even post that it sells for xx dollars on Amazon to justify their price. Even though they appear more tech savvy that doesn't mean you won't find deals from the uncaring or the unknowing.

If you've scanned your immediate area you can change your search radius and city to look even further. It can be worth a 500-mile drive if someone has a warehouse full of non-fiction books they want to dump. The search feature seems to be limited on radius but there is a manual trick you can use.

Type "book" in the search and then change your radius to anything after that search, the URL will look like the one below:

https://www.facebook.com/marketplace/denver/search/?query=book&latitude=39.7391&longitude=-104.98360001&radiusKM=161&vertical=C2C&sort=BEST_MATCH

Instead of latitude and longitude it might list your city instead. Either way, the **radiusKM=** is how far you want to search. The link above is 161 kilometers from Denver, Colorado. I chose this city because it's somewhat central, but you can change the 161km to 1999km in the URL, press enter, and search a large portion of the United States with it.

Don't forget people are sometimes willing to ship books to you. It might be worth the $5-$10 shipping for a textbook that will make you $50.

eBay

On eBay you'll be able to find bulk listings going for cheap. Sometimes these are all "duds" that someone has already gone through and sometimes they aren't. I've heard plenty of stories of someone buying a bulk listing and having it turn out profitable.

You can also arbitrage between eBay and Amazon, that is, you can buy cheaper on eBay and resell on Amazon or vice versa. If arbitrage excites you, it might be something worth looking into.

Gaylords

Gaylords are essentially huge boxes/bins and you can find these listed in a variety of places including Facebook Marketplace, Craigslist, eBay, and newspaper classifieds. They are typically offered by wholesalers or big book places trying to get rid of a ton of books. These massive bins are usually relatively cheap per book and typically sold by the pound or bin. Because they are big and heavy it can be a challenge going to get them or getting them to you. Some people will empty a gaylord into a small car or fill their vehicle to the brim with books.

For the person that can handle the logistics of acquiring these, this is something worth looking into. Having a bigger team that can help you go through them will expedite the process. Some sellers make all their money just from this sourcing method.

Craigslist and other sites

Craigslist is a classifieds marketplace online where you can find books, bins, and everything in between. It is always worth checking out the listings on this site. You can set up a filter/search that will automatically email you if it detects any new listings. It's a good idea to be aware of each post as it comes up in your marketplace as Craigslist is usually first come first serve. Search google for a guide on how to implement this alert.

Estate Auctions/Sales

Estate sales are where people go to collect some serious cash. Call ahead or check the listing to make sure they have what you want before going. An estate sale is usually from someone moving or from a death and everything left in the house is usually for sale. You can find things like mint conditions encyclopedias or other book sets. You can find rare / mint condition books that have been on shelves for decades. You can find massive libraries or collections that could have a higher acceptance rate than a thrift store. The possibilities are endless. You may be required to travel but it can be well worth it.

Garage / Yard Sales

If I left this source out, the Gary V fans would eat my heart. These types of sales will almost always have cheap books. How many or what you can find is part of the treasure hunt. Some will be amazing, some won't. Try to check the listing info ahead of time. It's better to plan a route before you go so you don't have to do too many "drive by bookings". Don't forget to download your scouting database in case you end up in the middle of nowhere without any service.

Advertising for Books

Marketing experience or background will be useful for this section. There are a ton of books on Internet Marketing that cover running ads on social media and other platforms. Let's keep this simple. If it makes sense to advertise to sell products, then it also makes sense to advertise to buy products to sell. Here are a few suggestions to advertise for books.

Running Ads

Almost all social media platforms have a way to pay to run advertisements on them. The restrictions for what type of ads you can run have gone up 1000% since inception but there are still legitimate ads that you can run that will bring you some business. Facebook Advertising, Google AdWords, and others also have either interest targeting, geographical targeting, or both and more.

Geographical targeting is important because if you're not willing to pay to ship books from outside your region, then why pay to run advertisements shown to people outside of your region? You can choose to have your ads displayed to a certain area by radius (recommended). You can also pick interests and other characteristics of an audience on some of these platforms.

The ad can be as simple as "I buy books" or "get cash for your used books" or "buying books in bulk" or something more specific to your business model. Do not forget to leave a way for them to contact you. For example, "Get cash for books, call xxx-xxx-xxxx for a free quote."

I know this is short and to the point but there are entire books written on advertising and even entire books written on advertising on just Facebook or Google alone, I have a few sitting on my bookshelf.

The takeaway is that you can target people by region and interests and run ads that only they can see. For more information on advertising, hit up google search or find a book or two on the subject.

Business Cards

Create business cards that serve as miniature advertisements with a way to contact you. You can pass these out to the managers or employees of the stores you thrift from. You can also leave these business cards on bulletin boards or other areas where they could benefit you. Perhaps drop a few in a library or the reading section of a Barnes and Noble. Be creative!

At a minimum your business card should include your name, contact information, and what you do or what you are looking for.

Example
Sir Booksalot, Book Collector
iwantyourbooks@booksplz.com
"I will buy your books from you in cash. Looking for mainly non-fiction but open to buying anything. Feel free to email me for a free quote."

Don't be intimidated by the creative process. There are places like

Cafepress, Zazzle, and Vistaprint that have ready to go templates to order from. All you need to do is enter your information.

Signs

I think almost everyone has been driving around and noticed a random sign stuck in the ground that says "Make money from home, call xxx-xxx-xxx" or "Will pay cash for your home, call xxx-xxx-xxxx". If you haven't, don't worry.

The reason why those signs are randomly all over the place is because they work. Making signs, flyers, or posters and putting them around town (especially by bookstores, places to read, or thrift stores) can attract some business. It may not be the most effective strategy, but it's a low-cost strategy that could pay off.

Direct Mailers / Email

If you have printed flyers or posters, you could also consider directly mailing these to stores you think may be interested. You may or may not get a response. If you're the bold type feel free to walk your flyer/pamphlet into these stores, ask for the manager, explain what you do, and leave them your card and pamphlet to get a hold of you if interested.

You can also try to directly contact store managers through email and explain what you do and ask them if they are interested. It doesn't hurt to try. Most of these stores have more books than they know what to do with and you would be doing them a huge favor by taking them off their hands.

CHAPTER 3: BOOK SELECTION

> *MAKING A WRONG CHOICE EARLY MAY LIMIT*
> *MAKING THE RIGHT CHOICE LATER. – JAMES FAUST*

A good rule of thumb is the more expensive and well put together a book looks or feels (high quality leather, high quality covers, nice clean pages) the higher chance of it being an acceptable book to sell. Sometimes just by picking up a book you can feel and sense the quality. These aren't always winners but a lot of them typically sell for more than $10 on Amazon and that usually puts you in the profit zone.

Books with higher initial Suggested Retail Prices (usually listed somewhere on the book) have a greater chance of selling for profit. A book that retails at $24.95 will have a better chance at returning profits than a mass market paperback that only sold for $7.95 to start with. This is not always true which is why we have scanning software and apps. There are a lot of expensive books that are duds.

You may want to avoid any mass market paperbacks, especially the fiction books. I've done a few tests in some stores that have their fiction books optimally set up for scanning. My average acceptance rate on fiction is about 1 in 200 scans as compared to the 1 in 20 rate I normally get in thrift stores. There is a greater chance of finding a keeper if the fiction book is hard cover but it's still well below average.

Don't scan fiction unless you have finished everything else and have nowhere else to go. Some of the accepts I've gotten from the fiction section were non-fiction books that were misplaced. If you have time it doesn't hurt to quickly browse over the fiction section to find misplaced books that could be worth money. The fiction section is optional but absolutely don't scan fiction if the books are listed at more than $1.50 each (cough goodwill) because you will end up wasting a lot of time.

You truly would have to have nowhere else to go and nothing else to do. Even if you pull a $100 book out of the fiction section every 2000 scans, you'd be missing out on the 100 non-fiction books worth at least $2 each you'd get doing 2000 scans in an appropriate section.

Worse yet, you could become delusional and develop an obsessive-compulsive disorder if you do find hidden treasure in the fiction section. It will forever cloud your vision as you dream of that one mega-find while you endlessly scan each fiction section "just in case" you find another one.

Numbers and time do not lie.

If you periodically find buried treasure, you will be outperformed money wise over time by the intelligent scanner. Even if you find a $10,000 book in there, over time they will still beat out your earnings if you continue to waste time in the fiction section on hopes and dreams. We are talking about earning enough to live off, somewhere between 30k-100k a year. Finding one $10,000 book, while as cool as that may be, still puts you 20k short of the goals of a semi-serious scanner.

Don't let your scanning become a fairy tale or you'll end up as a work of fiction yourself.

My Personal Scan Order by Section

This is the order I typically start with upon entering a thrift store:

1. Religious/Spiritual
2. Self-help/Parenting

3. Inspiration
4. Business
5. Autobiographies/biographies
6. Textbooks Hobbies (crafting, sewing, knitting, etc)
7. Music
8. Sports
9. Health/fitness
10. Animal
11. Fiction
12. Gardening
13. Cookbooks
14. Poetry
15. Classics

After the top 5 or so the sections become weaker having around 1-3% acceptance rates and don't really matter which order you do them in. When/if you get to these sections, you'll want to start honing your eyeballing skills because there won't and shouldn't be enough time to scan them unless you're out of stores.

In some of these sections you'll start to memorize titles that are never accepted, and you'll also start to recognize patterns or types of books that have no chance at reselling. "Chicken soup for the soul" is one of the famous non-sellers, so why scan 30 of them? Why scan the same Betty Crocker cookbook or a cookbook that has a new version every year where the old ones have almost no chance of selling?

Pay attention while you scan, you'll quickly start to see a pattern. If you truly have time to scan the entire book section, don't waste it blindly scanning, try to quickly glance at the book before scanning and guess whether or not it will be an accept or fail before you scan. **See how many you can get right!**

Although you will always miss some no matter how good you get at eyeballing a section, the time saved to scan better sections will more than make up for it. In my local thrift stores, some of the gardening / cookbook sections are bigger than all the other sections combined. It's like sifting through a mound of poop trying to find the gold ring someone swallowed. I don't care if you get out a stack of tarot cards, take a wild guess, perform a dance, or just scan them with your eyes but try to develop a method that works for you. Be smart about it.

While scanning the cookbooks section you're not looking for Betty Crocker's 2013 recipes, you're looking for Ming Yun's Secret Chinese Recipes. The more niche or specific the book is, the greater chance it has of being a resell.

Starting with Religious / Spiritual

A lot of people come running out of the gates thinking they are going to scoop up a bunch of deals and make a ton of money. Selling books online isn't quite that easy. But if time and resources were limited, where should you start? Some of you might not feel comfortable with what I'm about to say, yet, some of you will be thrilled to hear it.

The pathway to success in book selling begins with Jesus. You're probably thinking, "Oh great, another religious fanatic, why on earth did I choose this book to read?" But I'm not talking about saying a prayer, I'm talking about literally buying books about Jesus. But it's not just Jesus that will bring you profits, it's every type of religious and spiritual book you can find.

I've picked up books on witchcraft, exorcism, buddha, and a lot more. The stores I frequent are usually loaded with books on Christianity, but any book located in the spiritual / religious section of a store has great potential for profits. In the 30 plus stores that I regularly frequent, this is where I start every time because it has the highest acceptance rate. I call this getting gas, food, and hotel money. The first stop/first store is usually the break-even stop for the entire cost of my trip.

Bibles are usually priced up but sometimes the non-traditional looking bibles with names other than just "Holy Bible" can be worth a good chunk of money. Also watch for leather bound bibles, it takes time to look some of them up, but I paid 10 cents for one that sold for over $80 on Amazon. It didn't look like anything special, just a nice leather bound like-new looking bible.

Do not spend your time looking up cheap books that you think may be winners. It is better to buy 20 books for 10 cents each and look them up later. If you are wrong, it's only a $2 loss. A $2 loss is just one acceptable book and you can find one of those in less time than it takes to do the research on the other books.

The bulk of your books will probably come from this section. Sometimes I come out of a thrift store looking like a church group leader, but I don't care, because money is money. I feel like I'm doing a great service making these books available online because otherwise most of them would rot in these thrift stores.

The Truth about Textbooks

When I say textbooks aren't that great, I mean they are great, but they can be a hit or miss item. Textbooks can sell for $100-$500 per book if they are still being used in the current curriculum. Unfortunately, they are the first choice of the lazy looking to make a quick buck and in very high demand.

If you live near a college town your used bookstore on or near campus usually scoops up the bulk of these books paying prices you don't want to pay for them. It would be a hard sell to divert anyone from these bookstores unless you're willing to offer something similar. The textbooks that get dropped off at thrift stores are typically not the big $50+ books but rather the common books or junk books. Thrift stores, especially Goodwill, will raise the price of these books as high as $20 but there are some that you can still make $10-20 from.

The thing with textbooks is they are time sensitive. A book on Microsoft Windows XP isn't going to be in very high demand. You'll notice a lot of the textbooks at thrift stores are old and outdated. That doesn't mean you won't find a winner, but textbooks typically have a lower acceptance rate than the other popular sections.

I used to go for the textbooks right away while thrifting but even if I found 5 textbooks, I could have found 50 books in the other sections. Textbooks are still king but thrifting them might not be a good source.

Most of my textbook success came through Facebook Marketplace. I got books from people that took online classes or those that graduated and forgot to sell them before they left. It can be a little awkward going house to house picking them up or meeting random people. Some of them want to know what year you're in or talk about schooling so I just tell them the book isn't for me.

When I first started selling books it wasn't from thrifting. I landed about 10 textbooks from Facebook Marketplace that brought me over $500 in profits. I was so stoked that I thought I could expand my area of search and make a living from textbooks. But I quickly depleted the market and bought out all the available textbooks. Expanding my radius of search didn't help because it started to include college cities. People on the marketplace were matching Amazon prices so there was no way to flip textbooks for profit.

Moral of the story, treat textbooks like a gift when you find them, always spend a few minutes checking for them on FB, Craigslist, and in Thrift stores, but don't count on them to pay the bills.

The Children's Section

I absolutely despise the children's book section as a scanner looking to make money. The books are usually all different shapes and sizes and thrown all over the place. It's like the staff at most places gave up on that section too. Some books are destroyed. Some books will be acceptable but then you realize the sound box or special effect for the book is broken. I've even taken books, listed them, and had them returned without realizing there was supposed to be some token or accessory included with the book. Then there are books you swear should be worth money, like classic fairy tales, but are almost always duds.

I like to scan books from left to right and top to bottom with minimal effort and maximum speed. I don't even like it when the books in my regular sections change size so you can imagine how the children's section is a sore spot for me. I don't normally take the time but my girlfriend that I scan with loves these types of books. There are some pretty solid profits to be made for someone who can endure this chaos.

If you think about it, the children's section isn't really a true category because it contains all genres of books. It's like a repository of books made for young people thrown into the same spot. That means you'll be able to find children's books on religion, school, philosophy, and all the other categories that make money for the adult books. And you guessed it, fictional children's books are usually a low acceptance rate.

Be on the lookout for books that allow parents to have hard conversations with their children. Books on how to cope with certain diseases, disorders, puberty, or death are high in demand. Anything that can be uncomfortable or difficult for an adult to explain to a child will normally be a profitable book to sell.

Unless someone was bored, they likely didn't sort all the children's books into categories for you. It's not a bad idea to grab an extra cart, eyeball all the titles, and make a cart full of books you think could be winners for you to scan. You shouldn't have time to go through every book one by one, unless you have nowhere to go and nothing better to do with your time. The additional cart method above is a time saving option if you decide to go through the children books section at all.

Autobiographies/biographies

I got excited about this section when I started out but then reality eventually set in. The more popular the person it's about, the greater chance of it being crap to resell. There's no other way to really say it. Anything about Obama, Clinton, Princess Diana, JFK, Bill Gates, and other prominent figures, doesn't check out.

Once you recognize this, you'll start to see how you can rapidly get through this section and safely skip a large portion of it. By skipping through this section, you can sometimes get an accept rate higher than your average scan. Finding random obscure titles about holocaust survivors, individual stories about native Americans, and other races seems to be where the money is at.

The more niche or unknown it is, the better chance it has at selling. Some of the books I've picked up were so interesting I've kept them. When it's more about some random person's journey through a challenging time instead of about that actual person, there's usually a demand for that type of book.

If you remember supply and demand from school, the popular figures probably had millions of copies printed where some of these books may have way less in print and be harder to find used. Rarely do I get an "accept" on a New York Times Best Seller, there's just too many of them out there.

Classics / Rare Books

I'm not a hardcore classic or rare book finder. Most of the time I'm on a strict schedule and can't afford to do any research in store. When I first started, I didn't have massive travel schedules and time goals. I would finish an entire thrift store and have time left over for the classic book section. Half the books I found that were worth more than $100 came through regular ISBN and barcode scans, the other half were from taking a chance in the classic section.

There's usually a section or a shelf dedicated to classics where sometimes you can find first prints or other rare books. I paid 10 cents for a bible from 1902 that sold for $40 on eBay. I'm not going to tell you that you can't make a living finding classic or rare books but I do want to say that it requires a lot more book knowledge and research than the robotic scanning I get away with.

I don't rely on these sections because I'm there for guaranteed income. For the person that wants to spend time researching and learning what books to look for, there is money to be made, maybe even more than I'm making. Basic book scouting and sourcing is easy to master but becoming a book expert is above and beyond.

In most places you'll have the classics section to yourself. There are subreddits, blogs, and YouTube videos on classics that you can use to start learning about what type of books to look for. When you finish your regular scan, you can browse the classics section and pull out a few winners to pay for your kid's college fund.

CHAPTER 4: SELLING

SELLING IS NOT SOMETHING YOU DO TO SOMEONE, IT'S SOMETHING YOU DO FOR SOMEONE. – ZIG ZIGLAR

Pricing is something you'll want to pay attention to whether you send your books into Amazon or ship them yourself. Some of the fast selling books change price almost as fast as Bitcoin. Slow selling books aren't clear of any pricing danger either, there's always that one vendor that constantly undercuts you by a penny.

You must stay competitive to survive and there are a lot of tools that can help you do this. If you're Merchant Fulfilling, you can price your books accurately right away because those listings are live within 15 minutes. For Fulfilled by Amazon you'll want to wait until your books are checked into the warehouse before trying to competitively price. If you price them accurately before they are checked in, it's likely you'll have to reprice them when they are available for purchase.

There are a lot of ways to price your books. I have been using an app called NuPrice. The advantage of NuPrice is that it lets you quickly reprice items with a click. You can also filter and sort by date, name, SKU, and some other things.

There are some downsides to repricing software. NuPrice is limited to sorting features available through the API. Most software might have such limitations because it takes a lot of custom programming to add other features. NuPrice is relatively cheap compared to some of the other repricers so custom features may be hard to come by.

One thing you should look for is the ability to sort by the last repriced date. It makes the most sense to me that you should be able to target these listings specifically. I'm not aware of any repricers that currently have this feature yet. Most let you sort by list dates, but you don't usually reprice every book, so you end up going through everything again without knowing your last reprice date. If you find a piece of software that has this feature, please let me know.

Some vendors just have too many books to realistically reprice everything manually. There are a lot of vendors that use automatic repricing tools. These tools can cost 3-4x more per month more than a manual repricer. Automated repricing, when carelessly configured, can quickly send prices to the bottom. If you use automated repricers make sure your configuration doesn't let the price of your book drop below the profit you expect. If you let it reprice to the market without any restrictions, you could end up in an automatic robot pricing war and end up dumping books.

Sometimes you'll see someone undercut a listing by a $1 or more on a $10 book when a penny would have sufficed. Then you'll see someone else undercut that price and before you know it, the top 3 book listings are several dollars less than the rest. Your auto repricer will sell your book for you, but auto matching prices without rules can quickly net you some losses.

Amazon is trying to improve their free repricing tools. For me, it's hard to tell what's going on because Amazon doesn't seem to provide detailed information and control over what you're doing. It doesn't seem to separate between FBA and MF prices so clicking the "match low price" button can have some bad consequences.

If you ship your books into Amazon use a default price for all your books. Make sure that the price isn't so high that it gets flagged but also not so low that it gets bought before you can reprice. I use $24.95 as my default price and when I list books that are worth more than that, I'll change it to $55.95 or something I can remember to sort by.

Something I read suggested using $99.95 but almost all my books got flagged by Amazon and went inactive until I fixed the prices. That's a pain in the butt you don't want to have to deal with. You can find all the $24.95 prices later and reprice with NuPrice or some other software of your preference.

Repricing

After you've set a price you need to stay competitive. People aren't going to magically buy your overpriced books. Lower numbered sales rank means less volatility and more accurate prices. Anything with a sales rank of under 10,000 will sell quick so even if you're the third best price, chances are it will sell.

As you start to progress toward the higher numbered rankings, from 100-500k, you'll want to stay in the top 1-2 prices. When you move beyond 500k, especially into the millions, if you don't have the lowest price and the buy box, you will miss that once a month sale.

You've probably read somewhere that conditions don't really matter that much. For the most part this is somewhat true, but there are two areas where conditions will be the sole determining factor on whether your book sells. When you get beyond a million rank or the price of the book is more than $25, conditions are king.

If you're going to pay $50 for a book in acceptable condition, then why not pay $55 for a book in very good condition? As the price climbs the books in better condition start to dominate the sales preferences. What you'll come to learn is that the condition notes always mattered but when we are talking about a $10 book that is selling 500 copies a day, even the lesser conditions will still sell fast.

This changes when only 1-2 copies of a book are being sold a month. A lot of people think that buyers don't pay attention to descriptions, but this is inaccurate. There are some that don't pay attention to the condition. They are the ones who are leaving bad reviews on your account because the book had a scratch or was used when they didn't read the description and expected a new one.

When someone says people don't pay attention to the condition, what they mean is, the buyer doesn't care as much because it's a $10 book.

They're just going to read it and shelve it or donate it. This is not the case for rare, collectible, or expensive books. Condition is king, but the lower the price of the book, the less it matters.

The Importance of Book Rankings

Book rankings go from 1 (the most selling) to the least selling (somewhere beyond 20-30 million). Just because a book is high ranked (closer to 1) doesn't necessarily mean it's going to be worth more than a lower ranked book. Most of the time, if a book is selling a massive amount of copies it's going to be worthless or be worth only a few dollars profit. Fast sellers can be a good core of any book selling business because they usually have a steady price and a stable profit.

How often a book sells determines its sales rank. As the rank of a book decreases (goes into the millions) the rule of thumb is to get more money for the book if/when it sells because of storage fees. It seems that storage fees cause a lot of people to pass up profitable books or put ridiculous profit margin requirements on books in the millions before they'll take it. If you have a book that has a true rank and a history of selling, storage fees aren't as big of a factor as having sent in a dud that isn't really going to sell at all.

Let's just say on average it's going to be 10-15 cents a month per book. For a year you're looking at an additional $1.20-1.80 per book in storage fees depending on size and weight. This isn't as big of a deal killer as sending in a dud that will never sell.

When dealing with slower selling books, you SHOULD use something like Keepa to check sales history and activity. A book can jump from 30 million to 3 million rank from a good month of sales but may never sell a copy for a year or ever after that.

Checking the history on Keepa lets you see that this particular book in question sold 10 copies total in the last 5 years during one month this year and that's why it's sales rank has improved. It is up to you whether you think that trend has a good reason to continue or whether it's a fluke, but you can see it doesn't have a consistent sales history.

Too often you have 3-5 sellers on slow selling books undercutting each other hoping that their price is the lowest when the one person a year comes to buy the book. Having books ranked in the millions, even with high selling prices is like playing the lottery. You hope that your book will be the next one that sells.

If a book sells 1-2x every 6 months, it's likely to go to the lowest price booked on that day. It's also likely that someone will list another book within that 6-month period. It can be a frustrating game to play but eventually with competitive pricing your book SHOULD sell.

Make sure that when you use your ScoutIQ or whatever scouting software you use, that for books over 500,000 in rank you definitely start to take storage fees into consideration and raise the minimum profit margin you expect before acquiring.

Keepa graphs with premium access can play an important role in getting an accurate sales history on a slow selling book. This will let you make an informed decision on whether a book will sell and how long it might take.

The Buy Box

One of the biggest things for new sellers is becoming Buy Box Eligible. For new products, it seems almost everyone is eligible from the start, but for used products you need to "earn" the right to become eligible. If you go to "inventory -> manage inventory" in your seller account, there is a column in there that says, "Buy Box Eligible". This lets you know what products you have that are eligible for the Buy Box.

If you don't see the "Buy Box Eligible" column then it may be hidden from view. Look above your listings for a "preferences" button. Under preferences you can select which columns you want to see by default. The Buy Box is the single most important feature of Amazon whether you are selling FBA or FBM. Whenever you own the Buy Box you are the "add to cart" "buy now" option. If you don't have the Buy Box customers will have to click a separate link on the page to find you and other sellers.

Not having Buy Box Eligibility will reduce your visibility by 90% or more. This was a huge problem for me because I sold mainly new products on Amazon. For new products, the Buy Box usually went to whoever had the best price but for used products I wasn't eligible yet. Although I had cheaper prices than the seller with the Buy Box my listings received very little attention. Even with low visibility, some buyers will find you, and they will buy from you if you have the best price.

Getting Buy Box eligible is something you'll get over time after your sales and time selling in the category have reached some unknown number if you don't have too many negative reviews. Be patient, it will come. For some people this may take up to 6 months. For bigger sellers it might happen as early as 1-2 months. Think of it as Amazon making sure that you belong in the category that you're trying to sell in.

Every time you switch categories with used products, you'll have to earn the Buy Box eligibility back. You can earn the Buy Box faster by having a large inventory available with the cheapest prices. This is not the period where you try to make "bank" off your sales. This is the period where you sell as much stuff as you can so that you can get the Buy Box to increase your sales volume in the future. The Buy Box is significant so focus on serving your customers first by offering great support and the best prices.

What to do with "Duds"

No matter how good you are, you'll probably end up with some books that just won't sell. Hopefully you rescan all your books before you ship them into Amazon because once they are at Amazon it's hardly worth the expense of sending them back to yourself. Unfortunately, if you have duds that are in the Amazon warehouse, the best thing to do is pay the fee to have them disposed of or wait for a free removal period and get them all at once.

Sometimes you can price a book at a slight loss to try and sell it and save on the disposal fee. At the time of this writing the disposal fee is only 30 cents so you would have to be trying to save money on a lot of duds to really make an impact with this strategy.

Keep in mind that a dud is not always a dud. The Amazon marketplace can change quickly. I've brought home books that were "winners" and had them turn into "losers" before I shipped them to the warehouse. These books have their own special area called "rescans" in my warehouse. Some of these books turn back into "winners" within six months and some never do and end up in the burn pile but just keep this in mind before you get rid of your books.

There are some other creative things you can do with your "duds", but I really like the idea of hosting a burn party auction. There are a few ways to host an auction party but before you do this make sure you announce in some type of marketplace, social media, or your local paper that you are getting rid of xx amount of books to see if anyone is interested.

You can even add that you will be throwing them out if no one is interested to help get some attention. An example advertisement or post would look like: "Local bookseller cleaning out inventory. Thousands of books at great prices, mostly non-fiction, bulk pricing available. Any books left over will be thrown out, will sell all of them for xx dollars."

A burn party auction might be more fun. To host one, you can gather some of your friends or advertise on Facebook groups or around town that you're going to be auctioning off books around a bonfire. It's a good idea to have a live feed on Facebook or some other platform so people can make bids and participate from home. Start off by announcing the title and author, maybe reading the back cover or a paragraph and if no one bids on it, toss it in the fire. Repeat this process until all your duds are gone. You could also donate them, but if they end up at any of my thrift stores, I'm probably going to come find you and have a word with you.

Some people sort their duds by author or genre to sell them on FB Marketplace, eBay, Craigslist, or even Yard Sales. If you have 20 self-help books you could sell them as a "self-help" package. Or maybe you have 50 science fiction books, a collection of Star Wars books, or a bunch of books written by the same author to package and sell. Whichever way you want to try to package and arrange them is up to you. You can even sell them all together as bulk for cheap. As bad as it may sound, I would rather discard or burn the books than put them back into the marketplace where I may end up scanning them again. If you have a competitor you don't like, you could take them out of your local market and donate them to the source stores of your competitors to be funny.

AFTERWORD

This is the essence of the business of book selling. Where you go from here is up to you. I said this book was for the self-employed looking to make a part-time or full-time income from doing all of the work, but the reality is that this is all of the information you need to launch yourself from the S Quadrant (Self-Employed) to the B Quadrant (Business Owner) if you choose to.

There are many aspects of this business that can be outsourced. Using ScoutIQ you can set generic accounts up for other users that will show Green to Accept and Red to Reject without displaying any pricing or profit data. This would allow you to hire employees or contractors to go out with scanners and their own logins to find books at thrift stores or other sources for you. You could also hire people from different cities and areas around the country.

The price to ship books in bulk back to you is cheap enough to still make this a profitable model. You could even hire a manager that manages all your employees and contractors, recruits them, and takes care of the shipments for you. You could hire a warehouse employee/team that receives the shipments, scans the books, lists them, and ships them to Amazon for you. Every aspect of this business is nothing more than a job that you could hire someone to do. You will be amazed at how many people will go out and scan books for an hourly wage but won't do it for themselves as their own business.

You can play any of the roles you wish along the way from CEO to some type of small team leader. Think of all the aspects of doing the work yourself. You're literally running a shipping/fulfillment center, you're doing market research and product acquisition, you're in charge of the accounting and payments, you're managing listings and providing customer service, and so much more. Who can you hire to assist in all the different aspects of the business?

There are multi-million-dollar book selling businesses out there and there are individuals making a little extra side cash every week. Even if you want to remain solo, maybe there's a part of the business you don't like. For me that's sticker removal. You could hire some high schoolers or friends to prep the books for you. Maybe you like to just acquire the books, you could find a partner that wants to do all the listing and shipping for you. Or you can do it all yourself. Pretty neat business hey?

One thing people always ask for is a list of resources. I never like to put them in books because the resources can change or need to be updated frequently. I have made a resource page on my website that contains an equipment list, so you don't have to skim the book again to see what you need   to   purchase.

Here's a link you can check out to view all the articles that led to this book   and   the   equipment   /   software   list.

http://www.thomasvan.com/free-amazon-book-selling-course-2020

Thank you for reading and good luck to you!